CGP

GCSE

ICT

Information Communication Technology

Answer Book

The Answers

Section One — What Is a Computer?

Page 1

Q1 a) 8 bits.
b) A standard 8 bit binary code often used for storing text written in English or other Western European languages. E.g. a letter could be represented by 01000100.
ASCII=American Standard Code for Information Interchange.
c) The memory / amount of data that can be stored on a DVD-ROM — usually 8.74 gigabytes (on each side).
d) Data is information without the context to give it meaning.
e) If you get a computer to process data that's incorrect, the results will be meaningless. E.g. if you program a computer to work out the total cost of buying fifty McFly CDs (may they all warp) at £13.99, but you type in £139.9, you'll get the wrong answer.

Q2

Name of data type	Approximate size in bytes	Abbreviation
Byte	1	-
Kilobyte	1000	KB
Megabyte	1000 000	MB
Gigabyte	1000 000 000	GB

Q3 a) Yes (benefit)
b) No
c) No
d) Yes
e) Yes
f) No

Q4 For example:
i) Take up lots of space.
ii) Searching for records can take a long time.
iii) Only one person can access a given bit of data at a time.
iv) The data might get misfiled or lost.
v) Need to employ clerical staff to look after the filing system.
vi) Reports can be written, but only after looking at each relevant record and transferring information by hand. This is time-consuming and there is always the chance of human error.

Q5 a) Expensive, millions
b) Maintain, training, wasted (or lost)
c) Failure, power cut, lost
d) Files, information, hackers OR information, files, hackers

Page 2

Q1 A **computer system** is an integrated **system** of hardware and **software** that enables **data** to be input, then **processed** and the results communicated to the **user**.

Q2 B Data is entered at the input stage.
C The computer then processes the data.
A The results are shown at the output stage.

Q3 a)

Date	Code 1	Code 2
6th November 1973	061173	11061973
7th September 1977	070977	09071977
26th December 1908	261208	12261908
26th January 1988	260188	01261988
1st July 1947	010747	07011947
1st July 1946	010746	07011946
24th May 2002	240502	05242002

b) Code 1 doesn't include the century, so the computer might be confused, e.g., 24th May 1902 would be 240502, but so would 24th May 2002.

Q4

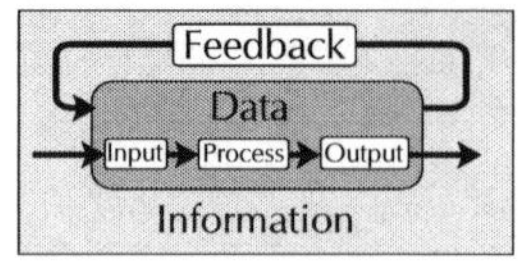

Page 3

Q1 a) Mainframes are... ii) ...the biggest.
b) Microcomputers are... iii) ...the most common type of computer.
c) Minicomputers are... i) ...in the middle.

Q2 The 1960s

Q3 Servers are used to run a small number of specialist applications continuously over a long period of time with very little human input. Because of this, they often don't have most of the bits that normally let you talk to the computer, such as keyboards and screens. They will often have more reliable hardware components, e.g. cooling fans and disk drives, than a typical PC to allow them to run more reliably for long periods.

Q4 When you need to run older systems alongside new systems, or when reliability is very important.

Q5 A PC.

Q6 a) ii
b) i
c) iii

Page 4

Q1 a) Disadvantage
b) Advantage
c) Neither
d) Neither
e) Disadvantage
f) Disadvantage
g) Neither
h) Neither
i) Neither
j) Advantage
k) Neither
l) Neither
m) Advantage
n) Neither
o) Disadvantage

Q2 a) LAN = Local Area Network
b) WAN = Wide Area Network

Q3 WANs are used by companies with more than one site, e.g. a supermarket.

Q4 Network file server.

Q5 For example:
Advantage: wireless networks mean you can connect from anywhere within range and they're easier to set up because there are no wires to plug in.
Disadvantage: wireless networks are much more expensive than cable networks / some people are concerned that there may be long term health risks from the radiation emitted by wireless networks.

Page 5

Q1 a) Line network / bus network.
b) Ring network.
c) Star network.

Q2 Bus network.

Q3 a) False
b) False
c) True

Q4 For example:
Star Network — Pros:
1. Performance in one part of the network is unaffected by events elsewhere.
2. Cable failure is less of a problem.

Cons:
1. Failure in the central computer causes the whole network to break down.
2. Uses more cabling, so it's more expensive.

Ring Network — Pros:
1. Cheap to expand.
2. Fast because data flows in one direction only.

Cons:
1. With lots of users the system becomes slower, as all the data is sent along a single line.
2. Failure of ring cable brings the whole network down.

Line Network — Pros:
1. Cheap, because it uses less cabling.

Cons:
1. With lots of users the system becomes very slow, as all data goes along a central line.
2. Failure of the central cable will bring the whole network down.

Q5 a) Star networks are used when a **large** number of **workstations** need to be connected to a central computer. Each workstation is connected **directly** to the central computer.
b) In **line** networks **data** is sent to and from the **file server** along a line of cable. All terminals are connected to this **central line**.
c) **Ring** networks are a bit like line networks, except that all the equipment is **linked** in a **ring**. Data flows around the network in **one direction** only.

Page 6

Q1 Physical, access and data security.

Q2 For example: keep a record of serial numbers, install alarms, use fireproof doors, lock windows, avoid putting computers on the ground floor, close blinds.

Q3 a) Son
b) Father
c) Grandfather

Q4 The son is the most **recent** backup of the **file**. When the next **backup** is made, this becomes the **father**.
When the next **backup** is made after that, the father **becomes** the **grandfather**. The grandfather file is **deleted** when a new son is **created**.
So if the **original** file is lost or **damaged** there are **three** backup files available.

Q5 a) Read-only files cannot be altered or deleted, only read.
b) Hidden files aren't usually visible to users (e.g. in Windows Explorer).
c) Archiving means copying or moving a file somewhere for long-term storage.

Q6 Access rights determine what a user can look at or modify on a system. For example, network managers can be given access to the software that controls how the network is run, while other users may be limited to certain applications, like e-mail and word processors.

Section Two — Parts of a Computer System

Page 7

Q1 Qwerty keyboard

The Answers

Q1 Qwerty Keyboard

Q2 e.g.

Type of keyboard	Where used	Type of buttons
Qwerty	offices	letters
Concept	shops and restaurants	symbols (or words)

Q3 Concept keyboard

Q4 When the **cursor** is over an icon, menu items, or the edge of a picture, the mouse buttons can be **clicked** or **double-clicked**. This sends a **command** to the computer. The button can also be **held down** to **drag** something across the screen. A mouse has an **optical sensor** that **detects** how the mouse is moved across a flat surface. From this, the computer can work out the **direction** and **distance** the mouse has travelled. This is used to move the **cursor** on the **screen**.

Q5 A touch-sensitive pad performs the same function as a mouse, controlling the on-screen cursor, but it takes up less space. The pad detects finger movement (instead of movement of the mouse) and taps (instead of mouse clicks).

Page 8

Q1 A joystick can be used to play computer **games.** The joystick can be moved a certain **distance** in any **direction**. The vertical and horizontal changes from its **rest** position are **recorded** by **sensors** to give a set of **coordinates**, which form the **input** data.

Q2 a) True
b) False
c) True
d) True
e) False
f) True

Q3 An advantage is that it's quick and accurate. A disadvantage is that the system only works if the OMR sheet is filled in properly.

Q4 The advantages to organisers and players are that it is a quick and accurate system that will easily record the choices made by players. It means that plays can be entered easily and this will permit the sale of more tickets. Players will find it straightforward to complete the OMR documents.
A disadvantage is that they need to make sure that the document is filled in correctly.

Page 9

Q1 Possible answers:
a) bar code reader (handheld or fixed position), touch screen.
b) digital video camcorder, digital camera, mobile phone.
c) 'traditional' buttons / control button to move or press, touch-sensitive screen, other touch-sensitive controls (e.g. iPod clickwheel).

Q2 a) 1
b) 7
c) 4
d) 6
e) 8
f) 5
g) 3
h) 2

Q3 Digital camera / camera phone / scanner.

Page 10

Q1 c) Central Processing Unit

Q2 a) Performs arithmetic.
d) Responds to control signals.
f) Moves things around in memory.

Q3 1. Load/Store — tells the CPU to move a piece of data from one place to another.
2. Arithmetic — tells the CPU to perform a mathematical operation.

Q4 Possible answer:
Control signals communicate to the CPU that there is an event happening outside its normal processing functions, e.g. a user moving a mouse. When a control signal is generated, the CPU pauses the current task and responds to the signal e.g. moving the cursor across the screen. The CPU then returns to the previous task.

Page 11

Q1

Output Device	Advantages	Disadvantages
Dot Matrix Printer	Cheap to run	low print quality
	Can print on continuous stationery	slow and noisy
Laser Printer	high resolution	expensive to run
	fast and quiet	can't use continuous stationery

Q2 a) False
b) False
c) True
d) True

Q3 Dot-matrix printers

Q4 b) produce permanent hard copies

Page 12

Q1 a) 2
b) 1
c) 3

Q2 Inkjet printers are a good compromise as they cost **less** to buy than other printers and produce good quality printouts. The print head of an inkjet device has lots of tiny **spouts** through which small **jets** of ink are **sprayed** onto the paper. In some printers, these are controlled by **crystals** while others **heat** ink so that it **expands** and pushes through onto the paper.

Q3 a) A printer buffer is memory inside the printer that stores the pages that have been sent to print from the computer but that are not yet printed.
b) Spooling is when the documents to be printed are temporarily saved onto the computer's hard disk in a queue. The printer can then take the data at its own speed. This frees up the CPU to continue processing data, allowing the user to get on with other tasks without waiting for the printer.

Q4 An inkjet printer would suit Sarah as it is affordable and produces good quality printouts. Inkjets have high running costs (e.g. replacing ink cartridges is expensive) when doing lots of printing, but Sarah will only be printing once every two months so this won't be a big problem. A laser printer would probably be too expensive for this amount of printing, while a dot-matrix printer is likely to have problems with poor print quality and colour reproduction.

Page 13

Q1 A Visual Display Unit is also known as a monitor and is used when visual information is needed but a permanent record isn't.

Q2 CRT monitors can give great picture quality, e.g. colour, brightness and resolution, often better than LCD monitors. The advantages of LCDs include they're compact and lightweight, use less power and are less damaging to the eyes.

Q3 Graph Plotters are specialised **printers** and are **accurate** and **precise** for drawing architect plans. A **flat-bed** plotter holds paper on a flat surface and a plotter **arm** moves over it from left to right. On the plotter arm is a **pen holder**, which moves up and down the piece of paper.

Q4 Jason should buy a flat-bed graph plotter — this would allow the printing of precision drawings and allow printing on much larger sheets. A laser printer could print high resolution, but not print on the large sheets that would be needed.

Q5 For example: speech synthesis can be used to help visually-impaired users. It can read out the content of documents, web pages and help the user navigate by reading menus, buttons, etc. Another common use is in automated phone systems, e.g. to guide the user through lists of options.

Page 14

Q1 a) Microfilm stores information by condensing hundreds of pages of information onto a standard roll of 35mm film.
b) Microfilm Reader.

Q2 a) It reduces the storage space required. Film lasts longer than paper.
b) It's expensive to use. If a microfilm is lost, a huge amount of information is lost.

Q3 Possible answers:
Lights
Bells / Sirens
Recording equipment

Q4 a) Output devices that are able to move and perform simple mechanical tasks.

Q5 Possible Answer:
A stepper-motor is where signals move the motor in a series of tiny but accurate steps.
A servo-motor is where the signal enables the motor to move continuously at high speed.

Q6 Hydraulic actuators are powered by **fluid** pressure controlled by the computer. They are **slow** but powerful.
Pneumatic actuators are like hydraulic ones but are powered by **air** pressure instead. They are less powerful but more **responsive**.

Q7 Possible Answer:
fast-moving automated production lines

Page 15

Q1 Random-Access Memory

Q2 Read-Only Memory

Q3 a) True
b) False
c) True
d) True
e) False
f) False

Q4 Volatile RAM stores data as **temporary** electrical signals and users should learn to **save** their work regularly as data stored in the RAM will be lost if the electrical power is switched off. ROM is **permanent** memory, so it's a type of **non-volatile** memory.

The Answers

Page 16

Q1 E.g.

Storage device	Advantage	Disadvantage
Hard disk	large data capacity	stored inside computer so not mobile
Optical disk	smaller and portable	easily scratched or damaged

Q2 **Hard** disks are usually found inside computers and are **rigid** circular plates that have been **magnetised**. **External** hard drives can also be connected if additional storage is needed. An **optical** disk stores digital data as small **indentations** on a reflective surface. A **laser-beam** moves across the surface of the disk to read the data.

Q3 E.g. optical disks have direct access to data making it quick and easy to find the data you want. Magnetic tapes have sequential access, making access time much slower.

Q4 CDs typically store around 650 Mb, DVDs store around 8.5 Gb and a 3.5 in floppy disk only stores 1.4 Mb.

Q5 Only once

Page 17

Q1 a goes with iii
b goes with i
c goes with ii

Q2 a) Digital Versatile Disk (or Digital Video Disk)
b) DVD-RAM, DVD±R or DVD±RW

Q3 Flash memory is used on storage media like memory sticks, memory cards and USB pen drives.

Q4 Advantages of flash memory cards and sticks include: very small and portable (so ideal for small devices like phones and digital cameras), very high storage capacity for their size, do not break easily.
Disadvantages include: easily lost, expensive, available storage capacities smaller than some other devices, e.g. hard drives.

Q5 Magnetic tape can back up large amounts of data. The data is written to and read from the tape in sequence, like a video or audio cassette. It's cheap but the access time is slow because the whole tape has to be read in order when accessing data.

Page 18

Q1 An operating system is the name given to the software that enables applications software and the rest of the computer system to work.

Q2 a) True b) False
c) True d) True
e) True f) False

Q3 a) Single program OSs can only run one program at a time — they allocate the entire system's resources to an application.
b) Multi-tasking means that the operating system can run more than one program at a time. The OS will share out resources such as available memory and CPU time between the different programs.
c) Multi-user means that more than one user can log into a computer. It's similar to a multi-tasking OS, sharing out available resources and providing each user with their own workspace.

Q4 Operating systems also maintain system **security**. **Programs** are prevented from accessing each other's **resources**. Users can only access resources (such as individual files) if they have **permission**. Extra users can be added to the system and their permissions restricted by the system **administrator**.

Page 19

Q1 A user interface is the way the user communicates with the OS, or other software.

Q2 Command-Driven, Menu-Driven, Graphical User Interface (GUI)

Q3 A **command-driven interface** presents the user with a blank screen while a **menu-driven** system displays a list of options organised under various **headings** or **menus**. The most popular type of system used today is a **graphical user** interface, which combines a menu-driven interface with **icons** to represent the main commands.

Q4 Windows, Icons, Menus, Pointers.

Q5 a, b, d

Section Three — Using a Computer System

Page 20

Q1 a) Input.

Q2 Optical Mark Recognition.

Q3 i) Questionnaire — manual.
ii) Sensor — automatic.
iii) Bar code reader — automatic.
iv) Computer-generated form — semi-automatic.

Q4 Possible answers:
a) 1) Faster and more accurate than manual systems.
2) Automatic data capture can be used in places that are dangerous to humans.
b) 1) Personal details can often only be recorded manually.
2) It is often cheaper to use manual data capture systems which require less specialist data capture hardware and software.

Q5 Possible answer:
Automatic data capture would be used in a nuclear reactor. It would be impossible for people to enter the reactor to collect data. The environment within the reactor would kill humans. This makes automatic data capture the only possible way of capturing data from within the reactor.

Q6 a) Bad
b) Good
c) Bad
d) Good
e) Bad
f) Good
g) Good
h) Bad

Q7 1) Check the form for accuracy and completeness.
2) Test the form on a small sample of people to make sure the information collected is accurate.

Q8 Possible answers:
a) 1) Better to explicitly ask for surname and forenames.
2) There is no explicit area to enter the post code.
3) The form does not ask for the member's telephone number.
4) The forms ask "When were you born?" rather than, "Date of birth:"
5) The space to enter the date of birth should be formatted in a manner that encourages the member to fill in the form in a format of dd/mm/yy, e.g. When were you born? _ _/_ _/_ _
6) The "What games console do you own?" question would have been better posed using tick boxes.
e.g. What games console do you own:
a) Playstation 3
b) X Box 360
c) Nintendo Wii
d) Playstation 2
e) Other
7) There are no instructions on the form to indicate a guardian's signature is only required if the member is under 16 years of age.
8) No lines given for the signature.
b) Any reasonable answer

Page 21

Q1 c) The data is the correct type and format.

Q2 Any three from:
Range check
Presence check
Length check
Check digit
Data type check

Q3 d) The same as the original data.

Q4 c) Double-entry

Q5 Possible answers:
a) They are automatic, making it quick and easy to spot errors.
b) i) Problems (errors) in the validation program allow mistakes in data entry.
ii) Validation checks only make sure the data is the right type. They don't check its accuracy.
c) i) Double-entry data verification is time consuming and expensive.
ii) Proof-reading relies on people and can't eliminate human error.

Q6

Name of Check	Description	Validation	Verification
Data type check	Check that the data entered is the correct type, e.g. if the field is a number field, text cannot be entered.	✓	
Proofreading	A second person reads the data entered into the computer system and compares it with the original data.		✓
Range check	Checks that the data is within a specified range, e.g. a person's birth month must be between 1 and 12.	✓	
Length check	Checks that the data is the right length, e.g. postcodes should never be more than 8 characters long, including the space.	✓	
Check digit	The final digit in a number calculated from a formula if the number is entered incorrectly the check digit will be wrong.	✓	
Double-entry	The data is entered twice by two different people. The system compares the two lots of data entered and highlights any differences.		✓
Presence check	Checks that data has been entered into a field and will not allow the field to be left blank.	✓	

Page 22

Q1 c) Files

Q2 b) Folder

Q3 A. False
B. False
C. True
D. False
E. True

The Answers

Q4 a)

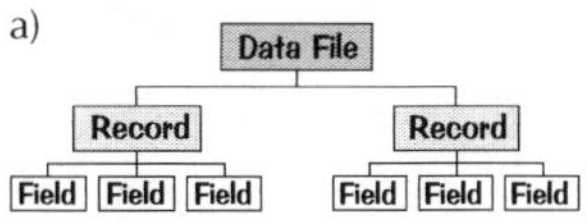

b)

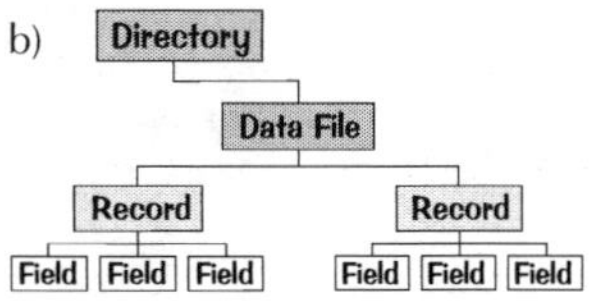

Q5 Possible answers:

a) A directory is a file containing information about other files and other directories. A directory tells the operating system and the users of the computer system where the files are, how big the files are and when they were created.

b) Fixed-length records take up a specific amount of space (characters) within a file. A fixed-length field of 20 characters will always take up exactly 20 characters of space within the file, e.g. in a fixed length field "surname" the surname "Smith" would occupy 20 characters worth of space, even though the last 15 characters of the field would be blank, and surnames longer than 20 characters would be cut off so the surname "Smyth-Worthing-Goodwood" would have to be shortened to "Smyth-Worthing-Goodw" to fit in a 20 character fixed-length field.

c) Variable-length records only take up the amount of space (characters) needed to store the field. The computer must be told where each field ends so more processing time is required to handle variable-length fields, but there is no wasted space, so the "surname" "Smith" would take only 5 characters. Fields can be expanded to hold the longest set of characters to be stored in a field, so the surname "Smyth-Worthing-Goodwood" would be held in full, using up 23 characters.

Page 23

Q1 a) A & 4
b) B & 1
c) C & 3
d) D & 2

Q2 a) Disadvantage
b) Advantage
c) Disadvantage
d) Advantage
e) Advantage
f) Advantage

Q3

Task	Type of Processing
Aircraft cockpit display	real-time
Booking seats in a theatre	interactive/transaction*
Cancelling a magazine subscription	transaction
Calculating the wages for a large company	batch
Looking at the availability of goods in a shop	interactive
Controlling traffic lights in a city	real-time
Producing 1000s of end of month customer bills	batch
Subscribing to a monthly video and CD club	transaction

* Booking seats in a theatre involves both interactive and transaction processing. Checking whether seats are available for a certain date and time uses interactive processing. Submitting the details and processing the booking (buying the tickets) is transaction processing.

Q4 Possible answers:

a) Interactive processing is when the computer's actions are controlled by the user, e.g. through a graphical user interface or through prompts given by the computer.

b) In transaction processing, the processing is broken down into individual actions, each of which can only succeed or fail. An example of a transaction would be the transfer of a sum of money from one bank account to another.

c) In batch processing individual changes to data (jobs) are stored up and all the changes are processed together. The processing occurs at regular intervals, usually in the evening or at weekends to avoid using valuable processing power during the working day.

d) In real-time processing, input data is constantly monitored and processed. Real-time systems are often used to control aircraft or manufacturing processes, like producing steel sheeting from molten metal, where an immediate response is required to modify the flight of the aircraft or the thickness of the molten metal.

Page 24

Q1 b) In sequential data access records are sorted into order.

Q2 Possible answer:

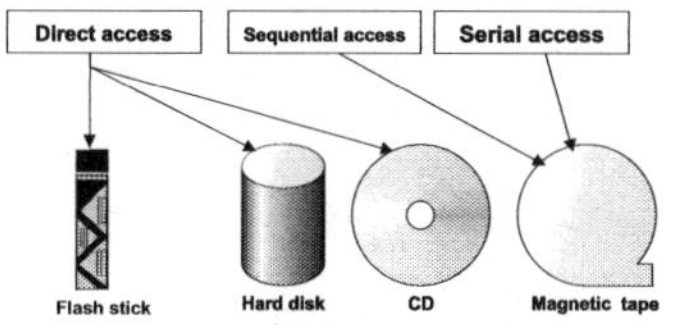

N.B. Sequential and serial access files can also be written to hard disk, flash sticks or CD, so lines joining these to the sequential and serial access boxes would be acceptable.

Q3 a) Direct.
b) Sequential and Serial.

Q4 b) The records that have changed are sorted into order.
c) The records that have changed are written to a transaction file.
a) The master file and transaction file are combined.

Q5 Possible answer:
Updating a direct access file is simple — the new or amended data is stored anywhere on the disk, and the computer's 'map' of the disk is altered, so it still knows where to find everything. Updating a sequential file is trickier. You first need to make an extra file called the transaction file. The transaction file contains just the records that have changed, and these are sorted in order of the key field. The original master file contains all the original data. The old master file and the transaction file are then combined by an updating program to make a new master file.

Page 25

Q1 c) Output device.

Q2 d) Speaker.

Q3 Any four of these possible answers, or other reasonable suggestions:
Text, sound, picture/graphics, graphs, charts, multimedia presentation.

Q4 A hard copy is a permanent record of information, usually printed or plotted on paper.

Q5 Possible answers:
Screen displays:
Advantages:
1) Information can be displayed immediately to users of the system.
2) Presentations can be enhanced by the use of sound and moving images.

Disadvantages:
1) The information cannot be viewed without going to a computer.
2) Some programs do not display a true reflection of how the information will look when it is printed out.

Hard copy:
Advantages:
1) The information can be taken away from the computer and read at a later date.
2) The information can be passed on to other people who do not have a computer.

Disadvantages:
1) Any mistakes in the information have to be corrected at the computer and the information must be printed again.
2) Only text and graphics can be displayed on hard copy. Neither sound nor animations are available to capture the reader's attention.

Q6 WYSIWYG stands for "What You See Is What You Get". This indicates that what you see on the computer monitor will be exactly the same as the printed hard copy of the information.

Section Four — Systems Analysis

Page 26

Q1 Systems analysis is the way that existing information systems are turned into new improved ones.

Q2 (clockwise from top right)
Carry out a FEASIBILITY STUDY.
ANALYSE the new system's requirements.
BUILD the new system.
Produce DOCUMENTATION for the users.
MAINTAIN the new system.

Q3 Firstly, there might be a problem with a manual system which could be solved by introducing a computerised system instead. Secondly, there might be difficulties if an existing computer system is unable to cope with the information processing demanded of it.

Q4 1) Interview users of the system
2) Analyse the results of questionnaires given to users.
3) Observe people using the system.
4) Study documents such as user guides and error reports.

Q5 b). But I'm sure they could be a) as well. And maybe even c). But mainly b).

Page 27

Q1 To analyse the requirements of a new system and help decide whether it's going to be worthwhile creating it.

The Answers

Q2 1. Decide on objectives for the new system.
2. Identify the hardware and software needed.
3. Carry out a cost-benefit study.
4. Make a recommendation.

Q3 a) False
b) True
c) False
d) True
e) False

Q4 As part of the **feasibility** study the systems analyst needs to make **decisions** about the types of **hardware** and software that will be used in the new system. These choices might be **changed** later on, when he moves onto the **design** stage of the system life cycle.

Q5 They answer the question: will the benefits of the new system be greater than the costs?

Q6 The findings are presented to the people who have the power to decide whether or not to proceed with the new system. These are often company directors or senior managers.

Page 28

Q1 a) Output
b) Input
c) Input
d) Process
e) Input
f) Process

Q2 a) False
b) False
c) True

Q3 It is important for the output of a system to be **user-friendly**. Users should only be shown the **information** that they need. It should be laid out in a format that they can **understand**. The layout of **output screens** and printouts should first be **sketched** in rough. The rough sketches should then be shown to the **user** to check they are alright.

Page 29

Q1 a) Top-down diagram.
b) By reading from left to right.
c) Er, no.

Q2 They show how data moves around a system, and what happens to it at each stage.

Q3 a) Shows a process.
b) Shows where the data is stored.
c) Shows where the data has come from.

Q4 No.

Page 30

Q1 How data will move through a system.

Q2 a) Magnetic disk.
b) Decision.
c) The error message is displayed and the receptionist must verify whether the input data is the same as the data on the original data-capture form.

Q3

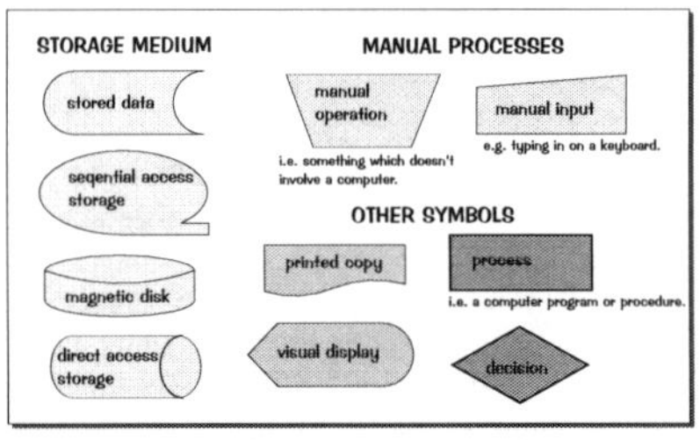

Page 31

Q1 System testing checks whether or not the system will work.

Q2 Normal data — anything that the programmer knows should work in the system.
Invalid data — is anything the programmer knows the system should reject.
Extreme data — data that deliberately tests the limits of information the field will accept (e.g length).

Q3 Acceptance testing checks whether or not the system meets the needs of the intended users.

Q4

Type of user documentation	Description
Installation guides	Explain how a system should be installed and programs loaded.
User guides	Give instructions on how to perform tasks using a system.
Tutorials	Short training manuals which explain how the system works.

Q5 Because they are intended to be used by experts such as computer engineers and programmers who will understand the more complicated terms and explanations.

Q6 1. When part of the system needs repairing.
2. When the system needs upgrading.

Page 32

Q1 Implementation is when a new system is built and introduced. Data from the previous system is loaded onto the new system.

Q2 Direct implementation, phased implementation, parallel implementation.

Q3

Type of implementation	Advantage	Disadvantage
Phased implementation	Time for the new system to be fully tested.	It can take a long time to introduce the new system.
Direct implementation	The benefits are seen as quickly as possible	Any bugs not picked up during testing could have disastrous effects.
Parallel implementation	Problems can be sorted out without affecting operations	All the tasks need to be done twice.

Q4 Once a new system is installed it will be **monitored** to see whether it's working properly. How well it's working will be regularly **evaluated** to check that the system still meets its **objectives**. Evaluation involves **observing** and **interviewing** users and studying printouts. The system might run into problems if the **workload** increases. If the system can no longer cope the **system life cycle** begins again.

Section Five — Text and Image Processing Software

Page 33

Q1 The complete sentence should read:
Modern word processors are more powerful...
a) ...because they can combine graphics, text and numerical information.

Q2 The missing words are:
processed, formatting, editing.

Q3 Word processing templates are documents with pre-defined layouts and formatting designed for a particular purpose, e.g. a memo. They designed so the user can quickly and easily adapt them to create their own documents.

Q4 E.g. Letters, memos, CVs, questionnaires, reports, newsletters, envelopes, labels.

Q5 a) Too many colours without any scheme.
b) Underlining does not highlight the most significant words, so is not helpful in drawing out the meaning of the passage.
c) Too many different fonts and effects.

Q6 Keep the layout simple. (Or other sensible answers.)

Page 34

Q1 The complete sentence should read:
Serifs are:
a) The little twiddly bits at the tops and bottoms of characters.

Q2 Serif: B & D, sans serif: A & C.

Q3 Highlight the text, select copy, put the cursor where you want the duplicate text and select paste.

Q4 Page margins fix how far from the side of the page the text starts and finishes.

Q5 The missing words are:
indenting, TAB, margins, line spacing.

Q6 a) 2
b) 1
c) 3

Page 35

Q1 The missing words are in this order:
tables, break up, columns, automatically.

Q2 a) A4
b) Portrait

Q3 a)

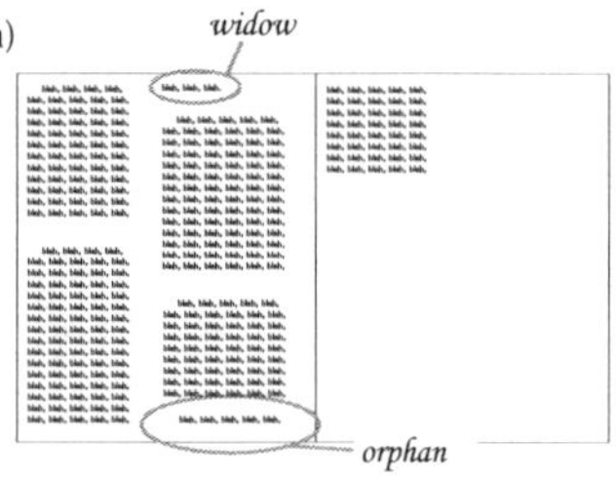

b) Possible answers:
Reduce the font size of the entire text, adjust the margins, move the whole paragraph to 2nd page, adjust widow / orphan control settings.

Q4 a) What You See Is What You Get.
b) A document will look the same on-screen as on a printed page.
c) E.g. To reduce the amount of memory / time needed to display the screen.

Page 36

Q1 a) They allow you to put blocks of text at the top and bottom which are kept the same on all the pages of a multi-page document.
b) Section Five — Text and Image Processing Software.

Q2 Search locates where a specific piece of text appears in a document, whereas replace can automatically change the text to something else.

Q3 a) i) True
ii) False
iii) True
iv) True
v) False
vi) False
vii) False
b) Good grammar depends on context and the software is not yet powerful enough to take this fully into account.

The Answers

The software is programmed with a limited number of rules, so there are many problems it won't recognise.

Q4 The missing words are:
readability, lengths, sentences, words, score. (Although "sentences" and "words" could also be the other way round.)

Page 37

Q1 A standard letter and information from a database.

Q2 The missing words are:
field, database.
standard letter, merges, inserting.

Q3 a) True
b) False
c) True
d) False
e) True

Q4 a) Importing means adding data created using a different software application e.g. putting a JPEG graphic into a word document.
b) That the imported data is saved in a format which the software you're importing to can recognise.
c) An embedded item can be edited within the word processor, but a linked item can't (you'd have to open the original file).

Page 38

Q1 Painting software:
- also known as pixel-based software.
- graphic saved as a series of coloured dots in a file called a bitmap.
- to edit the image you basically alter each dot individually.

Drawing software:
- also called object-based or vector-based software.
- image saved as coordinates and equations.
- image edited by manipulating objects.

Q2 a) Ready-made graphics which can be copied and used in your own documents, etc.
b) Lots of images are protected by copyright so using them without permission can be illegal.

Q3 The correct words are:
compressed, picture quality, not, decrease, file size.

Q4 a) Resolution means the number of pixels making up the image.
b) The more pixels used for the same area, the sharper / better quality the image — but the bigger the file.

Q5 a) Scanners convert photographs or hand drawings into digital images. The images are usually stored as bitmap or JPEG files.
b) Digital cameras capture real-life images and store them as digital images which can then be uploaded onto a computer. The images are usually stored as JPEG files.

Page 39

Q1 a) Select the graphic and then drag the 'handles'.
b) C

Q2 You could construct your image using different objects — remove the stick of celery from the original image and replace it with a judge.

Q3 a) flipping
b) rotating
c) recolouring
d) resizing

Page 40

Q1 a, c, d and f are correct. The other two are just silly.

Q2 a) Light
b) Dark
c) Neither
d) Neither

Q3 a) Graphic software can sharpen the image to reduce any blurring.
b) You can adjust brightness or contrast to edit images that appear too light or too dark.

Q4 A grayscale image is usually called black and white. But the colours and tones are changed to a relative shade of gray, including black and white but also many more.

Page 41

Q1 a) iii
b) i
c) ii

Q2 Marquee — isn't very useful if the shape you're trying to select isn't a rectangle.
Lasso — even with a steady hand it can take a long time to get the shape you want.
Edge Detection — programs sometimes get confused between the object, its layers and parts of the background.

Q3 You can use a copy and paste tool to duplicate objects in the image, or to copy in objects from other images. It's important to make sure that you only copy the object though, and not parts of the background as well.

Q4 Possible answer:
The clone tool can take a part of an image and copy it elsewhere in the image. When using the clone tool you don't have to specify how much of the image, or in what shape, you want to copy.

Q5 When you're cloning to remove objects, you place a **source** brush on what you want to copy, then **paint** somewhere else. The source brush will move in the same way as the mouse cursor. Anything under the source brush will be copied to the location of the cursor. The tool can be used to copy simple **patterns** such as **grass** or the **sky**. This is particularly useful when replacing an object with a single colour would look wrong. The clone tool can also **repair** small areas of the image, such as facial **blemishes** or bits of landscape left behind when an object is **removed**. By cloning lots of small pieces, you can even construct **new shapes**.

Page 42

Q1 Computer-aided design.

Q2 The missing words are:
designed, processed.
calculations, cost.
materials, components (or the other way round).
simulate.

Q3 a) True
b) False
c) False
d) False
e) True
f) True
g) False

Q4 Advantages:
CAD lets you create designs very quickly.
It's QUICK to change designs.
Good systems can produce high-resolution images.
Simulations help you design better products first time round.
Disadvantages:
CAD software is EXPENSIVE.
CAD software is COMPLEX so users need A LOT of training.
CAD systems REQUIRE powerful hardware.

Page 43

Q1 The correct words are:
professional, frames, text, graphics, better, specialised.

Q2 a) Frames
b) They allow you to move and resize text and graphics easily.

Q3 Taking the labels clockwise starting at the top left, the missing words are:
frame-based, position.
frame, drag.
delete, move up.

Q4 You can create professional looking documents.
The layout is easier to change than with a word processor.
It's easier to control the number of pages.

Page 44

Q1 a) Text frames can be linked together so that text which doesn't fit in one frame will flow through into the next.
b) A graphics frame can be set so that when it is positioned on top of a text frame, the text automatically positions itself around the graphic instead of being covered by it.
c) Layering frames means you can put different frames over the top of each other and move them back or forward between layers. E.g. text frames could be place on top of a graphics frame to add labels to the graphic. A box could then be drawn and sent to the back to make a background for the graphic.

Q2 a) False
b) True
c) True
d) True and False are both acceptable answers.
e) True
f) True — fascinating eh.

Q3 a) Files containing the basic layout and format for a standard document.
b) Any suitable answer, e.g. newspaper, school newsletter, etc.
c) Possible answer:

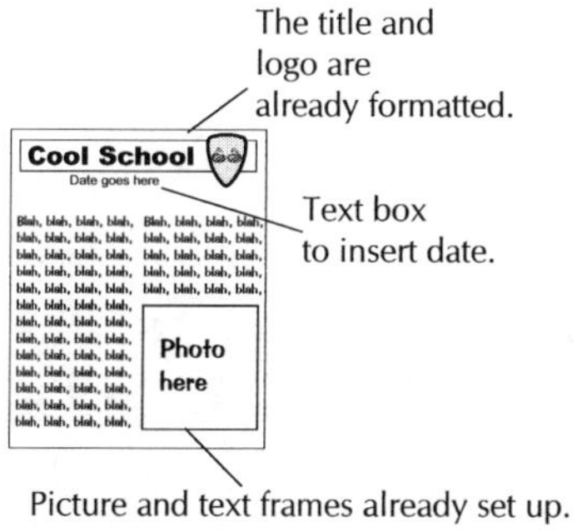

The Answers

Q4 a) With handwritten or word-processed slides / transparencies.
b) E.g. It's easy to muddle up the order. The speaker may have to cover up information they don't want the audience to see yet. The presentation may look unprofessional.

Q5 Advantages:
It produces professional-looking presentations.
Presentations CAN BE USED MORE THAN ONCE.
It's easy to edit and adapt presentations.
Use of multimedia can make it EASIER to get people's attention.
Disadvantages:
Hardware, e.g. LCD projector, can be expensive.
It is easy to get carried away by the technology and produce badly-designed slides.

Section Six — Spreadsheets and Databases

Page 45

Q1 a) False
b) True
c) True
d) False
e) True
f) False

Q2 a) Yes
b) Yes
c) Yes
d) Yes
e) No

Q3 Cells

Q4 a) Numerical data (incl. times and dates), text data and formulas.
b) No.
c) i) Numerical value of zero — should be -56
ii) fine as it is
iii) fine as it is
iv) numerical value of zero — should be 100

Q5 Text string is the ICT term for a piece of text or a sequence of text characters.

Page 46

Q1 a) Rows
b) Title
c) Field names
d) Cells
e) Columns

Q2 A data validation formula is a formula used by a spreadsheet to determine if the contents of a cell are valid (e.g. if a number is in the right range).

Q3 a) For example: Alter font, colour, size, and use italics or bold type.
b) Conditional formatting is where the format of a cell is altered if the cell's contents meet certain conditions, e.g. you could set the cell to turn blue if the number inside it became greater than 100.

Q4 a) Comma-Separated Variables
b) When the data is saved, a comma is inserted between each piece of data in a row, and a line break is inserted at the end of each row. It is transferred easily because it is always in the same format.

c) By using copy and paste — although if you try and edit the spreadsheet then the spreadsheet program will still load.

Page 47

Q1 a) =B3+C3+D3 or = SUM(B3:D3)
b) He can copy the formula in E3 and paste it into the other cells in the E column.
c) =E3+E4+E5+E6+E7+E8+E9+E10, and it should go in cell E11. Or, he could use =SUM(E3:E10).
d) Relative.
e) Absolute cell references are formulas that always need to refer to one particular cell — you don't want the computer to change it. Relative cell references use data which is in the same place relative to the answer cell.
f) $B$5

Q2 =E3/$E$11*100 or equivalent (e.g. =(E3*100)/$E$11)

Page 48

Q1 d)

Q2 a) Yes
b) No
c) Yes
d) Yes
e) Yes

Q3 a) iv
b) =IF(C2<£10,000, "no","yes").

Q4 A look-up table is a table of information that is accessed from elsewhere (e.g. another part of the same spreadsheet). It means you can, say, convert an account number into a customer's name without having to trawl through a big table / database.

Q5 Look-up tables may be more convenient for companies with large data lists, as they speed up the process of finding information.

Page 49

Q1 The correct order is: d, c, f, b, a.
Step e is useless, but in case you're wondering, it's an archaic Dutch word for "quack".

Q2 Legend.

Q3 a) Scatter graph.
b) Bar graph.
c) Line graph.
d) Pie chart.

Q4 a) Scatter graphs show the relationship between two sets of data and may have a trend line to show the relationship clearly.
b) Bar graphs have categories on the x-axis and values on the y-axis. They are used when each category is discrete (i.e. separate from others).
c) Line graphs are like bar graphs but are used when the data on the x-axis is not in categories.
d) Pie charts show the contributions of categories to a total.

Page 50

Q1 a) True
b) False
c) False
d) True
e) False

Q2 The key field contains an item of data that is unique to that record — no records have the same value in the key field.

Q3 Speed — you can search through databases incredibly quickly.

Q4 A title / description of its contents.
A data type.
A format.

Q5 Any reasonable answers — for example:
a) Chingford
b) 78
c) 78.93
d) 23-08-02 or 23/08/02

Q6 Coding is the use of a few characters to stand for a bigger entry (e.g. M to indicate Male, F to indicate Female). It helps to reduce the file size of the database — it takes up less memory because it uses up fewer characters. It also reduces the amount of time / typing it takes to enter data.

Q7 Possible answer:
The data in flat-file databases is organised into one table, which can be viewed by opening one data file. They can be created using all database programs and most spreadsheets. Relational databases store the data in separate tables and files. All the data's linked together by key fields and a data management system (DBMS). The DBMS controls who can access what. Relational databases are used a lot in large organisations.

Page 51

Q1 Simple queries tell the database to look for records that meet just one condition.

Q2 a) Bob Beckham
b) Tony Stevens
c) Felicity Smith
d) Bob Beckham
e) Eric Walker

Q3 a) Wildcard searches.
b) When you want to search for records containing part of a name rather than the exact name (e.g. all records ending in 'ing').

Q4 Boolean (logic) operations.

Page 52

Q1 A report is the result of a database query that is intended to be seen by someone else.

Q2 a) Record-format
Useful if you want to view each record on its own. Suitable for using as reminder slips, or mail-merge letters.
b) Column-format.
The data is displayed in a big table with all the information shown under the field headings. More useful if you want to compare values in particular fields across different records.

Q3 Not all database software allows you to format the text, so exporting into a word processor or desktop publishing package gives you more options. Alternatively, you might want to export data to do a mail merge.

Q4 Possible answer:
They could use a complex query to search for all the customers that had previously rented more than, say, 3 Tim Crewes films. The customer details could then automatically be combined with mail-merge documents to produce personalised letters and address labels.

The Answers

Q5 a) Pro
b) Pro
c) Con
d) Pro
e) Con
f) Con

Q6 Good examples of a database report are: a, d and e.
b is not because the report would be the same as the original data entered.
c is not because it is such a small number, that you could easily find the information yourself.

Section Seven — Measurement, Control and Simulation

Page 53

Q1 Sensor

Q2 c) Large amounts of data have to be collected.
d) The data has to be collected over a very long period of time.
f) Data has to be collected every 1/10 of a second.
g) Temperature has to be monitored inside a large deep-freeze.

Q3 Digital signal
Analogue signal

Q4 Possible answers:
Light sensor — used to detect when it is dark enough to turn a street light on.
Analogue.
Radioactivity sensor — used to ensure the radioactivity of power rods in a nuclear reactor are within working levels.
Analogue.
Sound sensor — used to ensure that noise levels along aircraft flight path are within agreed levels.
Analogue.
Infra-red sensor — used as part of a burglar alarm, activated when someone breaks the beam by walking past it.
Digital.
Air pressure sensor — used to detect a drop in air pressure in an aircraft cabin and activate oxygen masks.
Analogue.

Q5 a) Before an analogue signal can be used by a computer system it must be converted into a digital signal. Analogue to digital converters are used to convert analogue signals into digital signals. An analogue to digital converter often forms part of the interface board that connects an analogue sensor to a computer.
b) CSV file stands for 'comma-separated variables'. This means the file contains variable length data fields separated by commas. CSV files are used because most spreadsheet, database and word processing applications know how to read CSV files, allowing the data to be exported to any of these applications for analysis.

Page 54

Q1 The logging period is the total length of time data is collected for.
The logging interval is the time between one measurement and the next.

Q2 $$\text{Number of readings} = \frac{\text{Logging period}}{\text{Logging interval}}$$

Q3 The **logging** period of a system is determined by the **length** of time it takes the process being monitored to be **completed**. The logging **interval** is usually determined by the length of the logging period. The shorter the process being monitored, the **shorter** the logging interval. Monitoring the growth of plants will require a logging **period** of weeks with **daily** logging intervals. Monitoring the progress of a chemical reaction that completes in a matter of seconds would require a logging period of less than a **minute** with a logging interval 1/10 of a second or less.

Q4 A questionnaire — No
Forms would be used to ask questions and record the answers.
The number of cars — Yes
Sensors would give accurate readings and operate continuously over the whole period.
An opinion poll — No
Forms would be used to ask questions and record answers.
The acceleration — Yes
Sensors would provided accurate information for the short period.
The temperature — Yes
Sensors would operate in this environment which is dangerous to humans.

Q5 Possible answers:
1. Data logging equipment can be used where it would be dangerous for humans to go, e.g. in a nuclear reactor, the crater of a volcano, the bottom of the sea, etc.
2. Data logging equipment can operate over very long periods of time (months or years) — humans might forget to take readings. Very short periods can also be recorded — humans would find it physically impossible to take readings every fraction of a second.
3. The intervals between measurements can be very accurate when using data logging equipment, ensuring uniformity of the logging interval and allowing accurate readings to be taken at the end of each interval.
4. Because it is automatic, data logging is continuous. The equipment does not stop to take breaks or sleep.

Page 55

Q1 Computer-controlled.
Dedicated.

Q2 a) Dedicated control systems carry out a pre-programmed set of instructions.

Q3

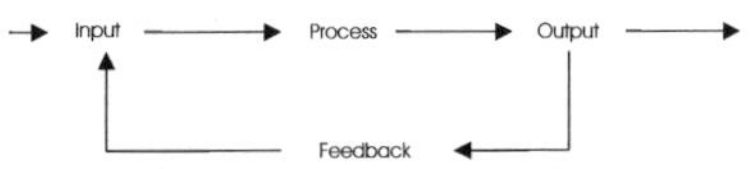

Q4 a) a digital to analogue converter, (DAC).
b) an analogue to digital converter (ADC).

Q5 a)

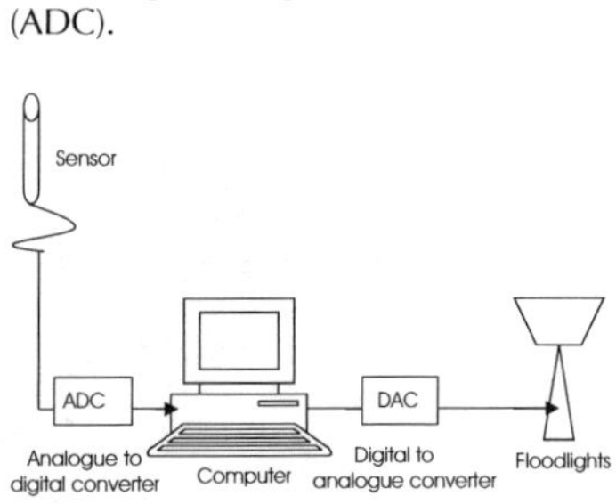

b) The **light-dependent resistor** (sensor) senses the level of natural light and produces an analogue signal (voltage). The signal from the sensor is fed into an **analogue to digital converter** (ADC), which turns the voltage from the sensor into a digital signal which can be read by the computer.
The **computer** processes the signal from the sensor and as the light drops it increases the output signal to the floodlights.
The output signal from the computer is digital and must be passed through a **digital to analogue converter** (DAC). The DAC regulates the voltage to the floodlights.
The **floodlights** receive their power from the DAC. As the signal from the computer increases, the voltage from the DAC increases and the floodlights glow brighter.
c) If the sensors were placed below the floodlights, the light from the floodlights would produce a false reading within the sensor. This could cause the computer to turn the floodlights down when it was dark. Once the lights were down, the sensor would correctly register that it was dark and the computer would turn the floodlights back up again. So the floodlights would fade up and down in the dark rather than providing a constant light.

Page 56

Q1 b) Do it once and remember.
d) Teach and learn.

Q2 d) Teach and learn.

Q3 Advantages:
Cheaper to operate than paying people wages.
Don't get tired or make mistakes.
Carry out tasks that humans can't or won't perform.
Disadvantages:
Can't think for themselves and so can't respond to new situations as well as humans can.
They are expensive to buy.

Q4 Possible answers:
Infra-red sensors can be placed around the robot's working area. If the infra-red beam is broken the robot will stop what it was doing and remain stationary.
Metal guards can be used to protect the robot's working area. Digital switches placed on the guards will indicate when a guard is opened. The robot will stop and remain stationary when a switch is activated.
Pressure pads can be placed on the floor around the robot's working area. Pressure on the pads indicates that something or someone has entered the robot's working area. The robot will stop and remain stationary when a pressure pad is activated.

Q5 a) The temperature sensor detects the temperature within the greenhouse and produces an analogue signal that is passed through an analogue to digital converter to the computer.
The computer determines how far the windows should be open and transmits

The Answers

a signal to the electric motors via a digital to analogue converter.

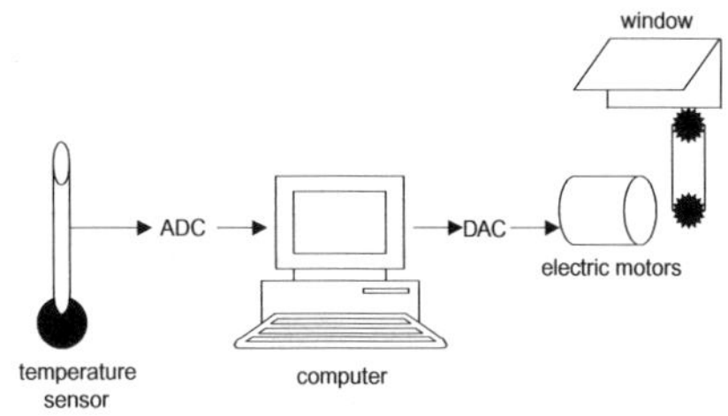

b) A dedicated control system to feed plants three times a day could be constructed from a small pre-programmed set of instructions which would activate a small pump to pump nutrients to the plants, at three fixed times a day, e.g. every 8 hours.

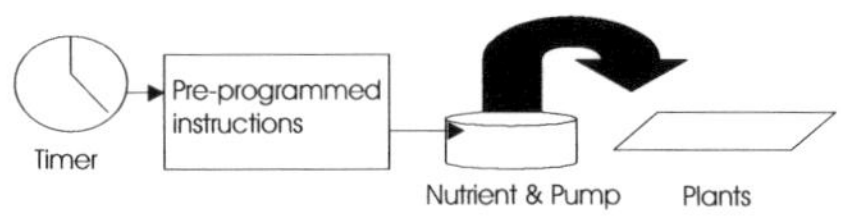

Page 57

Q1 Computer, automated device, sensor.
Q2 Feedback loop.
Q3 The computer drives the pump to pump oil down the pipeline.
The pressure sensor senses the pressure of the oil in the pipe.
If the pressure drops the speed of the pump is increased. If the pressure increases the speed of the pump is decreased.

N.B. This is an example of a feedback loop.

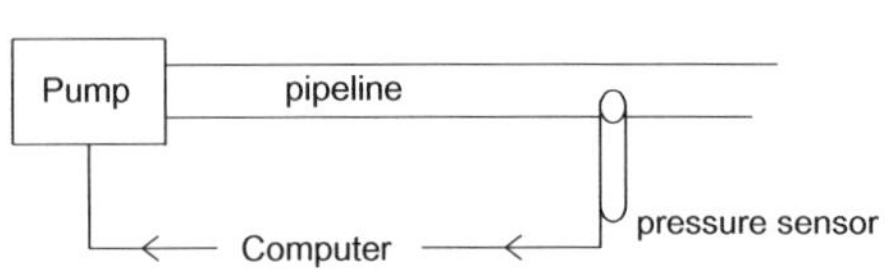

Q4 a) Draws a line tracing all LOGO commands following this one until the next PENUP command.
b) All the LOGO commands that follow this command will NOT draw any lines. This will be true until the next PENDOWN command.
c) Rotates to the right by X degrees.
d) Rotates to the left by X degrees.
e) Moves forward X units.
f) Moves backward X units.
g) Repeats the LOGO commands inside the square brackets X times.

Q5 a) The shape is an arrow. 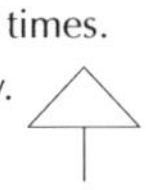

Q6 A computer program is a list of commands that the computer must perform. Before the commands can be carried out by the computer they must be translated into machine code (binary codes that the computer understands).

Page 58

Q1 a) A computer model.
b) iii) A simulation.
Q2 Computer, rules, equations
Q3 1) Spreadsheet.
2) Computer-Aided Design models.
3) Virtual Reality models.
4) Expert systems.
Q4 Advantages:
1. Dangerous situations can be simulated. For example, teaching aircraft pilots how to crash-land a plane using a flight simulator.
2. The model can be used to make predictions about how the real thing would behave under extreme circumstances e.g. how much weight could a bridge hold before collapsing.
3. Running a simulation is often cheaper than testing the real thing e.g. destroying a real bridge.
Disadvantages:
1. The model might not be an accurate representation of the real world — so the simulation might give misleading results.
2. The behaviour of objects in the real world is very complex, because of their interaction with variables like temperature, wind speed and other objects. It can be very time-consuming to produce a model that simulates all these variables.
3. Some models and simulations are expensive to build and run.
Q5 Expert systems are built on a knowledge bank — a database of facts, questions and possible answers. The computer asks the user a series of questions. The answers given by the user are looked up in the knowledge base. The knowledge base will return either another question to try to refine the information given by the user or it will return a fact which will help answer the user's question. When the computer has gathered sufficient information from the questions asked of the user it will suggest a solution to the user's problem.
Q6 For a virtual reality system to provide a realistic environment for users the sound produced by the system should be as realistic as possible. Stereo sound systems are commonplace in modern computers, but more realistic surround sound systems can create an audio environment where sounds come from every direction, as they do in the real world.
Tactile feedback plays a large part in the realism of the system. If the users can feel the items within the virtual reality model the model becomes more believable. In expensive, complex virtual reality systems gloves connected to electrical motors have provided the sensation of touch. On a simpler, every day level, many games pads now include built in rumble packs. When used with games the controllers vibrate and produce effects for various situations within the game, e.g. a controller will vibrate to simulate the effects of cars hitting walls in race games.

Page 59

Q1 e) Formulas.
Q2 Spreadsheets use **formulas** to create **models**. The formulas describe the **rules** of the model. By changing the **variables** in the spreadsheet, the model can be used to answer **what-if** questions.
Q3 Graphs and charts.
Q4 a) = B2 + C2 + D2 *or* = SUM(B2:D2)
b) The value in C2.
Q5 What-if analysis is when the user changes input values (variables) in a model to see what effect this will have on other figures, like the company's profits. What-if analysis is often used to calculate the effect on a company's profits of, say, changes in wages or the costs of raw materials.

Page 60

Q1 a) Output
b) Input
c) Output
d) Input and output
Q2 Advantages:
1. It's safer to teach pilots to fly in a simulator. It's also a safe way to practice emergency drills.
2. Time in a flight simulator is cheaper than time spent flying a real aircraft.
Disadvantages:
1. The simulator can't replicate every experience of flying a plane, for example the G-forces felt under extreme acceleration.
Q3 For example:

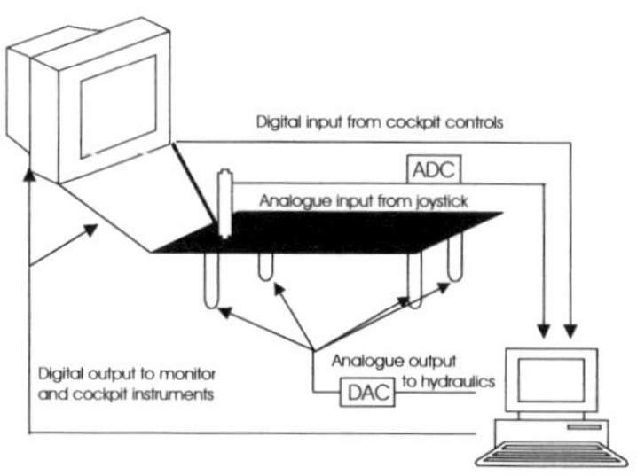

Q4 E.g. Light levels
Cabin pressure
Noise levels
Q5 a) Real-time processing
b) The pilot will look at the instruments and the display, feel the movement of the simulator and make adjustments to the flight controls (the throttles, joystick etc.) This input will change how the plane behaves and thus affect the output of the instruments, screen and hydraulic pistons.
c)

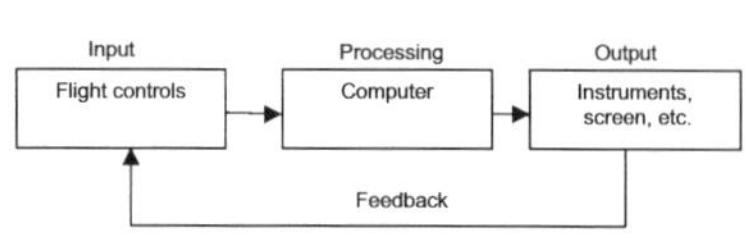

Q6 a) A flight simulator computer game can only mimic the experience of flying a plane. Although the game program may be sophisticated and obey the rules of an aircraft in flight, the controls for the aircraft will be minimal, perhaps employing a joystick for the main flight and using the computer keyboard for other actions, like setting the plane's flaps. The computer monitor may go some way to showing the user the view from the cockpit and some of the sounds of flight, but there is no movement within the room to simulate the feeling of flight.
b) Virtual reality can enhance the illusion of flight by providing a complete visual

The Answers

re-creation of the cockpit that the user cannot see beyond. Feedback to the controls and seat used by the virtual reality system will add some level of movement to the simulation, but may still fall short of the full experience.

c) A full flight simulator provides the nearest experience to flying as it encapsulates the user in an environment which is as near a duplicate to the aircraft cockpit as possible. Movement to the cockpit will simulate most of the movements of an airplane and the visual and audio stimulus will be close copies of the real thing.

Section Eight — The Internet

Page 61

Q1 a) ii) A set of computers connected by high-speed communication lines.
b) iii) The United States Government.
c) Connect military computers together.

Q2 a) WWW — World Wide Web.
b) ISP — Internet Service Provider.
c) ISDN — Integrated Services Digital Network.
d) ADSL — Asymmetric Digital Subscriber Line.
e) WAN — Wide Area Network.

Q3 Possible answers:
a) Hardware — modem and PC and cables.
Software — Anything that will allow Internet access — e.g. dial-up networking software, a browser or e-mail software.
b) For example:

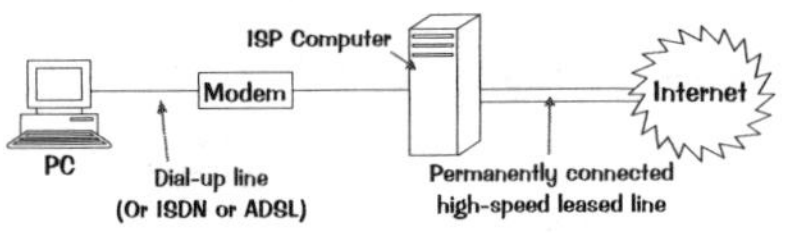

Q4 Possible answer:
The World Wide Web is a set of interconnected web pages. Users can move from one page to another. A collection of web pages that are linked together and held on a single computer (a web server) are called a web site. Web sites can be held on computers anywhere in the world.

Q5 Possible answers:
a) The older Internet connections used normal analogue telephone lines and so could not transfer very much data (only 64 Kbps at best). The newer digital lines are specifically designed for carrying digital signal and have a wider bandwidth, making them around 128 times faster than the old connection (about 8Mbps).
b) Because the lines that we use to connect to the Internet can carry much more data, people use the Internet for downloading music, watching film clips and videos and sharing whole files. It used to take hours to download a single song or clip.

Page 62

Q1 The address book.

Q2 i) You can send email using a mobile phone's connection to the Internet.
ii) Digital TV also allows people to send e-mail.

Q3 i) Run a virus-checker on your PC
ii) Do not open e-mails that look suspicious or are from people you don't know.

Q4 Attachments.

Q5

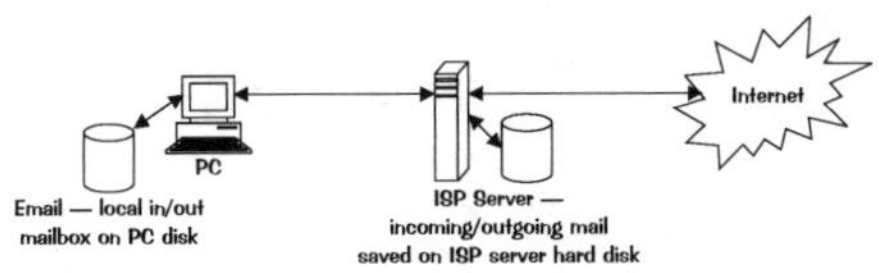

E-mail is composed on the local PC and stored in the e-mail client's "outbox". When the PC connects to the ISP the e-mail client transmits the contents of its outbox to the ISP server. The e-mail client also receives any incoming mail from the ISP server. Users can then read their new mail. The ISP server stores e-mails from e-mail clients in its own outbox area on the server hard disk. At regular intervals the ISP server will transfer the contents of its outbox to the Internet. The ISP server will also collect e-mails from the Internet that are addressed to its users, and store them until the user connects to the server again. E-mails are then transmitted to them through the client.

Q6 Possible answers:
Speed: e-mail is very quick to send
Cost: it can be very cheap to send messages all over the world.
Ease: you can send the same mail to lots of people very easily.
Access: the sender and the receiver of mail both need access to Internet.
Viruses: they can be transmitted by e-mail.

Q7 Web-based email does not use a local e-mail client to **store** and forward **e-mail**. Users of a web-based e-mail read and compose new e-mail via a **web browser**. The e-mails are retrieved **directly** from and transmitted directly to the users' inboxes and outboxes on the ISP server. As web-based email does not use a **local store** on a client PC, e-mail can be read and written from **any** PC.

Page 63

Q1 c) Uniform Resource Locator

Q2

a)	neither	g)	omelette
b)	omelette	h)	web browser
c)	web browser	i)	omelette
d)	omelette	j)	neither
e)	omelette	k)	web browser
f)	web browser	l)	neither

Q3 Domain type Country code

<http://www.cgpbooks.co.uk/ICT/default.htm>

Protocol Domain name Path HTML file name

Q4 Possible answer:
a) A search engine is a web site that gives access to a database of keywords found on web pages. When a user searches for a word using the search engine the engine's database is searched and the URLs of web pages with matching words are returned in a list.
b) Portals are web sites that usually give access to a range of services. You can either search for something with a search engine, or follow links to services like e-mail or online shopping.

Q5 a) AND, e.g. 'revision AND computer'. Matches will contain both the word 'revision' and the word 'computer'.
b) OR, e.g. 'revision OR computer'. Matches will contain either 'revision' or 'computer' (or both).
c) NOT, e.g. 'NOT computer'. Matches will not contain the word 'computer'.

Page 64

Q1 Possible answers:
a) A hyperlink on the Internet connects different parts of the web and can take you from one place on the web in your web browser to another. Of course, hyperlinks aren't just for the Internet — they can be used to link to any file, anywhere, even on a local computer.
b) To make text hyperlinks stand out from the normal text on a web page, the text of the hyperlink is a different colour to the main page and the hyperlink text is underlined. Most web browsers change the cursor when the user moves the mouse over the hyperlink, e.g. the cursor may change from a pointer to a hand.
c) Hyperlinks that have already been visited by a user are often displayed in a different colour to the hyperlinks that have not been visited. E.g. hyperlinks that have not been visited are often coloured blue; hyperlinks that have been visited are often coloured red.

Q2 E.g.
Bookmarks (or Favourites).
History.
Back / Forward buttons.

Q3 E.g.
i) Another page on the same website.
ii) Another file on the same computer or on a different (linked) computer.

Q4 Web browsers keep a record of the web pages they have visited. This is called the history and it allows the user to quickly return to a web page or site recently visited.

Q5 a) File compression reduces the size of a file. Various compression techniques can be used, e.g. repeating characters/bytes in the file can be removed, the original file can then be reconstructed from one of the characters/bytes and the number of times it appears. Because a compressed file is smaller than the original file it takes less time to download.
b) images, sound, video, animations.

Q6 A cache is an area of storage set aside to store regularly used information. Web browsers can save web pages that have already been visited by the user and store them on the hard disk or flash memory. When the user selects the URL for that page again the browser simply loads the page from the memory, which is much quicker than retrieving the page from the web.

The Answers

Q7 a) i) c ii) g iii) h iv) a v) d
vi) f vii) j viii) b ix) e x) i

ii) Back — takes you to previous web page.
Forward — (works if you've used back) takes you forward to the next web page.
Stop — stops downloading or transmitting information.
Refresh — reloads the current web page.
Home — takes you to your home page.
Search — takes you to a search site.
Favourites — displays web pages that you've marked as favourites.
History — displays all the web pages you've visited for ages (like about a month). They're sorted by when you looked at them.
E-mail — Options for sending or checking e-mails.
Print — Prints current web page.

Page 65

Q1 Hypertext Mark-up Language

Q2 E.g. Web page editors, Word processors, Desktop publishing software

Q3 E.g. Javascript or ActionScript (for Flash applications)

Q4 a) Clarity of appearance: the title is easy to read but the rest of the text hard to read, especially because it is against a dark background and bits have been skewed. The four links at the bottom of the page aren't properly in their boxes, so they're hard to read too. The page is too dark overall to be clear.

b) Relevance of information for visitors: the page isn't that helpful or welcoming to first-time users — there's only the membership form link and no mention of first-time users in the main text. Regular users aren't going to want to look at this page because it's got nothing new on, and it will take a long time to load because of the graphics.

c) Text should be informative (or interesting, e.g. funny). The text on this page, if it can be read, doesn't really say much. Plus there are spelling mistakes in it: membership and dinghies are both spelt wrong.

d) This site looks pretty awful. It's too dark, and looks really cheap and tacky. Some attempt at design has been made by using a rough drawing of a sailing boat for the links and text, but it's been poorly done.

Q5 a) Dynamic content can change every time a web page is opened. Things like a date / time display, or a hit counter (the number of visitors) are refreshed every time you log on to a web page. Dynamic content can also generate brand new pages depending on information that the user enters on previous pages, like further recommendations when you're shopping online.

b) Interactive content responds to movements the user makes with the cursor or keyboard. Films, sounds and songs are all examples of interactive content — they can be stopped and started by the user.

Page 66

Q1 Unauthorised users (hackers) can intercept data transmitted over the Internet.

Q2 a) 'The key is in the decryption of this message'.

b) It's called an encryption algorithm. It's the rule that was applied to each character in order to encrypt the information.

Q3 a) A computer virus is a computer program designed to copy itself and infect other computers, sometimes corrupting or deleting files in the process.

b) A secure site is a website that uses encryption to keep information you enter — and information it sends back to you — private.

Q4 a) Hacking is the illegal access of computer systems. Hackers access computer systems without permission with the intent of reading, modifying, deleting or adding to the data stored on the system.

b) Organisations can deter hackers by:
i) Encrypting files.
ii) Providing users with passwords and ensuring that they are changed regularly.
iii) Using hacking detection software

Q5 When the user finds something they want to buy, they add it to a virtual shopping basket. When the user has selected all the items they want to buy, they enter a checkout page where the prices are totalled and the user is presented with a bill (the user can add or delete items from their shopping basket at this point). The user then has to submit some personal info including credit card details to purchase the items in their basket.

Q6 E.g. a hospital might use an intranet to hold patient records. These records would be available to doctors and nurses in the hospital and would allow GPs to view records of patients registered with their practice. To ensure that only authorised users access the site, users would be given a login name and password and would enter these on connecting. An intranet can also be physically isolated so that it can't be accessed remotely (e.g. from Internet).

Page 67

Q1 Any three of:
On a discussion board, through an information resource (like wikipedia), by writing or commenting on a blog, or through a social networking or gaming website.

Q2 A "hive mind" is the combination of lots of users' expertise on a subject. It means that the information available on a subject has been approved by many people who know something about it.

Q3 Information resources like wikipedia demonstrate the hive mind, as do web pages and discussion boards aimed at solving problems.

Q4

Advantages	Disadvantages
1. Regular contributors can be given special privileges and roles within a community.	1. It's possible that you can end up spending more time online than in the real world.
2. A community of contributors can produce lots of accurate and useful information.	2. Privileges can be abused and can ruin the community for other users.
3. People enjoy interacting with each other and having a sense of community.	3. There's not an easy way to check that people are who they say they are.

Q5 A blog (short for WebLog) is a web page consisting of entries (usually text and images) 'posted' by a single user for other users to read. It's like an online diary or journal. It can be used by people travelling, or who have moved away from friends or family, to share their thoughts and experiences with each other.

Page 68

Q1 Lots of people **contribute** content to websites on a regular basis. It's quite difficult to keep track of **what** is being added, and **who's** adding it. Most user-generated content can't be **verified** — there are no specific **rules** to follow to make sure content is **accurate**. Most websites rely on other **users** to edit their content. And of course, some information is just rubbish — just because it's on a **well-known** website doesn't always mean it's reliable.

Q2 a) Copyright protects the rights of the original artist or author of a piece of work. It is generally illegal to use material that someone else has produced, especially if posting it publicly on the Internet, without getting permission or at least acknowledging the person who holds the rights.

b) Libel is the name for statements about organisations or individuals that are not true and are damaging to their reputation. This can be an issue for discussion forums online, and users can be sued for libellous comments (although they can be removed from the Internet very quickly).

Q3 There are no regulations to force website hosts to monitor the content produced by users. On the really big UGC websites, this would be an almost impossible job anyway as there are there are so many people uploading content.

Q4 Some websites produce written policies covering copyright and acceptable usage that users have to agree to before they are allowed to post anything. Chat rooms and discussion boards within specific websites usually have administrators who monitor the postings and can remove anything that breaks the rules. They may also use programs or filters to automatically remove postings that break particular rules.

Q5 Statements 2, 3 and 5 are true.
Statements 1 and 4 are false.
The main problem that this causes is that no one's really sure where responsibility ultimately lies for content. If hosts are making an effort to monitor content it shows that they are trying to take responsibility for what is posted on their

The Answers

site. Unfortunately if a website is monitored like this it means that the ultimate responsibility for the content itself lies with the website host.

Page 69

Q1 A thread is an original question or comment and all the corresponding posts or responses to it by other users.

Q2 They have administrators and moderators to keep an eye on how people use the site and what they post. Users have to register and create a username and password, as well as agree to some terms and conditions before they can start posting.

Q3 Spam is the name generally given to unwanted communication. It takes the form of nonsense posts, adverts that haven't paid to advertise anywhere officially, or repeated posts intended to fill up boards and slow them down.

Q4 Trolling involves posting inappropriate or unsuitable material. Trolling can affect message boards by offending or upsetting users.

Q5 1) Immediately.
2) Connected to the Internet.
3) Personal, Intrusive.
4) Webcam (although technically both are true).

Q6 They have responded by closing down most open access chatrooms, and by creating functions to allow users to keep lists of contacts that they know. You can reject or remove people that you don't know if they try to talk to you.

Page 70

Q1 Any five from:
Email, Instant Messaging, posting blogs, discussion or shared interest groups, sharing files or website links, chatting over webcams or making voice calls.

Q2 Any four from:
A photo or picture, where you live, where you go to school, what music or films you like, your pets, your hobbies or interests, what sports you play... and so on.

Q3 It wouldn't be sensible to include:
Your address, your telephone number or any private details (like bank stuff).

Q4 The easiest search is by name, but you can also search by a username, email address, a school you went to, or by common interest.

Q5 c) Confirm they know each other.

Q6 Advantages:
You can keep in touch with people all over the country / world.
Large networks can be used to raise awareness about appeals or charity events.
Disadvantages:
It's still possible for personal information to be at risk.
Employers or other interested parties can find out a lot about you from what you think might be innocent information — and you don't always know who's looking at your profile.

Page 71

Q1 Most of the online audio and video content is provided by amateurs.

Q2 Professional companies provide:
Audio — in the form of singles and albums to buy and download, as well as online interviews and podcasts.
Video — movies can be bought and downloaded from the Internet. Television episodes will often be available to view for free online for a certain period after they have been broadcast.

Q3 1) Yes 2) No 3) Yes 4) No 5) No
6) Yes 7) No (well, it's a bit excessive).

Q4 Possible answer:
Citizen journalism is the use of amateur footage captured on a mobile phone or digital camera. It provides first hand footage of an event that news or sports journalists may wish to cover.

Q5 A vlog is a video equivalent of a blog. Instead of writing and publishing online, the log is recorded on video and then uploaded.

Q6 Anyone can upload audio and video content using websites like Youtube and Google Video. Some people will use sites like these to illegally upload copyrighted material, e.g. television episodes. The sites can take some action, e.g. remove items that breach copyright, and possibly take action against the user, e.g. banning them from the site. But they can only do this when they are aware of the items, e.g. when a user flags a video. Because there's so much content being uploaded it's not possible to remove these problems entirely.

Page 72

Q1 Online software is supposed to create the same experience on the Internet as your normal software does on your computer.

Q2 With online software a user can create documents and allow other online users to view them to provide feedback. It also allows documents to be produced in collaboration — multiple users can edit a document at the same time with an online chat window allowing them to communicate while they work. The software can keep a list of all the changes that have been made and which user made them.

Q3 Early online software could only perform pretty basic word processing functions. You could edit documents online but only the text — images and spreadsheets etc. couldn't be changed.

Q4 Ultimately people hope to create an entire operating system online. Currently there are versions of entire Office packages available online, so you can edit or create pretty much anything and share it with other users, store it online, post it to a website, and so on.

Q5 The **layout** of online software isn't quite as **user-friendly** as you might be used to on your own computer. Compared to loading documents direct from your **hard disk**, it can sometimes **take time** to access them online. There can be problems **uploading** and **downloading** files if they're saved online, and sometimes files don't **save** properly and can become **corrupted**. There are also some **size** restrictions on online files as well as the general **security** issues with saving something on the Internet.

Section Nine — Computers in the Real World

Page 73

Q1 Electronic Point Of Sale

Q2 Electronic Funds Transfer at the Point Of Sale

Q3 a) A check digit is an extra digit added to the end of the original number. It is calculated with a formula that combines all the other digits. If you recalculate it and get a different answer, you know the number's been misread (or you're no good at maths).
b) Check digits are used as part of bar codes in an attempt to make sure that the bar code is not read incorrectly on a product.

Q4 a) The product code from the bar code on each product.
b) The price of each product obtained from the supermarket database.
c) E.g.
1. The product code of each product in the shop.
2. The price of each product in the shop.
3. The stock level of each product in the shop.

Q5 When a product is scanned at the checkout the product code is transmitted to the shop's computer.
The product code is used to locate the product in the shop's database.
The stock level of the product is decreased by 1. When the stock level of any product falls below a minimum stock level the computer automatically generates a request for new stock which is transmitted to the shop's suppliers.

Q6 When you pay for something with a card you're asked to use a Chip and PIN (Personal Identification Number) device. The device connects to a banking system and the customer enters their PIN. The device then validates the number. Some shops still use the older method of checking a signature against the one found on the back of a card.

Page 74

Q1 E.g.
1. Cheque processing.
2. Automatic Teller Machines (ATM).
3. Home banking.

Q2 a) Magnetic Ink Character Recognition.
b) Cheque number, sort code and account number.
c) Magnetic ink reading is almost 100% accurate and the characters can be read even if the cheque has been damaged or the magnetic ink characters have been written over.

Q3 E.g.

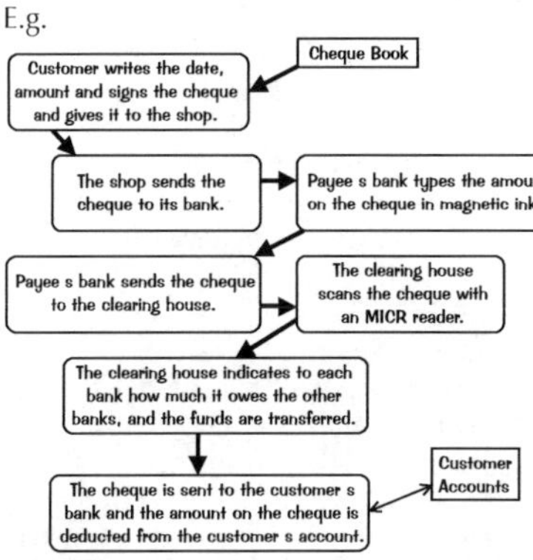

The Answers

Q4 Possibilities include: card number, name, country code, expiration date and the maximum amount allowed to be withdrawn in a specified period.
N.B. To prevent fraud the customer's PIN is not stored on the card. The PIN number is stored in the bank's database against the customer's account number.

Q5 This type of check is a verification check, as the entered PIN is verified against a known value.

Q6 Apart from a computer, you would need a modem and equipment to connect to the Internet e.g. telephone line. You would also need an account with an Internet service provider and a web browser that supports data encryption to access the bank's online banking facilities.

Q7 Advantages:
Paper costs are lower (cheques, statements, etc.)
Fewer branches required (less rents, rates, electric bills, etc.).
Disadvantages:
High cost of sophisticated security systems.
Internet fraud by hackers gaining access to accounts.

Page 75

Q1 a) Any three of the following:
e-mail, multimedia presentations, intranet, EDI, document scanners (Digital Copiers)
b) Electronic Data Interchange
c) An intranet is a mini-internet run over an organisation's network. It can include normal internet services as well as making internal documents available online to all people connected to it.
d) E-mail is an essential part of a paperless office because employees can then send written information to their colleagues and other organisations, electronically, without using paper. (There are other methods such as direct file transfer, but e-mail is very quick and convenient).

Q2 Advantages:
- Paper costs are lower.
- There is no storage space required for filing cabinets to store paper, so a smaller office can be used, saving money on office rent.
- Searching for documents on a computer system is quicker than searching for paper in a filing cabinet.
- Paper can be misplaced or lost.

Disadvantages:
- The computer equipment required by a paperless office is expensive to buy and maintain.
- The information stored on the computers could be read by computer hackers.
- Failure of the computer system means no work can be done in the office.

Q3 Electronic data interchange allows organisations to transfer electronic information over high-speed communication lines. Orders for goods can be transmitted as electronic data to the company supplying the goods. That company then sends an electronic request for payment via the EDI system. No paper passes between the two companies. Payment for the goods will be achieved by an electronic transfer of funds from one company's bank account to the other's.

Q4 Videoconferencing uses a video camera or webcam connected to a computer, which is connected to a telephone network or the Internet.

Q5
- The office can save money on travel costs as meetings can be held without leaving the office.
- No time is wasted travelling between meetings and the office.
- International organisations can save money on hotel bills as meetings with staff in different parts of the world can take place without having to travel to and stay in another country.

Page 76

Q1 a) Computerised Management Information System
b) Any two of: Pupils' names, dates of birth, addresses, attendance figures or exam results.
c) On a computer database, indexed by admission numbers.

Q2 a) Optical Mark Recognition
b) The teacher completes an OMR attendance sheet, which is then input using an OMR device.
c) Portable keypads can be used as an alternative to OMR.

Q3 Advantages, possible answers:
1. Schools spend less time producing management information.
2. This means more time can be spent on teaching and learning.
3. Easier to back up data.
4. Easier to analyse data and generate statistics.

Disadvantages:
1. Financial cost to the school.
2. Teachers need to have access to computers and the data.

Q4 Computer-aided learning uses **software** to generate on-screen **learning materials** and computer-aided **assessment**. The pupil's ability is assessed and a learning programme of an appropriate **level** is provided. The pupil therefore gets an **individualised** learning programme. Another element of an electronic classroom is an interactive **display** board. All the computers in the class are **connected** to the board, which is at the front of the classroom. It means **everyone** can watch a **presentation** by one pupil. The board can also **convert** the teacher's board notes into a **computer file** which can be saved and used again.

Page 77

Q1 a) Any three of: The driver's name, address, date of birth, the year they first qualified to drive and the vehicles they are qualified to drive.
b) Any three of: The car's make, model, colour, engine size, registration, year of first registration and owner / registered keeper.

Q2 a) This changes the traffic lights after a fixed length of time. The length of time never varies and the system loops round, changing the lights after each time period has elapsed.
b) These use sensors to detect the number of vehicles passing through the lights. The time cycle for the lights uses the feedback from the number of cars passing through the lights to alter the length of time the lights stay green each way.

Q3 A light (or infra-red) sensor.

Q4 The camera takes pictures of speeding cars and the car registration number is recorded on the picture. The car registration number is unique to the car and is used as the key to the vehicle database held by the DVLA. The registration number can be used to locate the car in the DVLA database and find the registered owner / keeper of the car.

Q5 Sensors at the entrances and exits of car parks are used to calculate how many spaces are left in the car park. This data is sent to signs next to nearby roads, which update their display in real time — so motorists know when the car park is full.

Q6 Geographical Information System

Page 78

Q1 Possible answers:
Playing games, keeping home accounts on spreadsheets, writing letters in word processors, communicating with friends and work through e-mail, using education software, using the Internet.

Q2 A modem or equivalent (hardware).
A connection to a telephone line or equivalent (hardware).
An Internet browser (software).

Q3 a) Infra-red beam, noise sensor, pressure sensor.
b) Any two of: siren / loudspeaker, flashing light, signal to police station.

Q4 An embedded computer is one where the input, process and output devices are all contained inside the machine that it's controlling.

Q5 E.g. Microwave, oven, video recorder, washing machine, DVD, CD player, dishwasher, tumble-dryer.

Q6 Possible answers:
1. It might be possible to control all household devices from a single central control and then connect to this control via the Internet.
2. The central control might be able to store details of products that have bar codes. These could be scanned when a product is thrown away. The computer could then automatically re-order foodstuffs that are running low.

Page 79

Q1 a) Weather data, e.g. wind speed, rainfall, air pressure, hours of sunlight, etc.
b) Data collected from many sensors is collated and processed by a single computer to produce the map, often with the help of a geographical information system.
c) Information about the current weather system is fed into a supercomputer, which uses mathematical models and information about previous weather patterns to predict the evolution of the system.

Q2 It means the estate agent doesn't waste time showing round people who turn out not to like the property. It means people can

The Answers

quickly see what a house is like and decide whether they are interested, without spending time and travel expenses.

Q3 Estate agents collect **details** of a property and give prospective **buyers** a written description of it. It's often hard for them tell what the property is really **like** and whether it's worth **viewing** the property. One way of solving this problem is for estate agents to use **digital cameras** and interactive software to produce **virtual tours** of the property.

Q4 Software can be used to take a digital image of the room and then manipulate it (e.g. by adding furniture and changing colours) so customers can be shown what the room might look like.

Section Ten — Computers and Society

Page 80

Q1 a) On the computer used by one particular user only. (It is OK to install the software on more than one machine if it's for the same user, e.g. a work and home computer, but the software must not be run on both computers at the same time.)

b) On a network where other users will have access.

Q2

Year Law Introduced	Law
1984	Data Protection Act
1989	Copyright, Design and Patents Act
1990	Computer Misuse Act

Q3 To copy the file without the permission of the owner or the copyright holder.

Q4 The data protection act allows data subjects to see the personal data an organisation holds on them.

Q5 1) Data mustn't be processed unless there is a specified lawful reason to do so.

2) Data must only be obtained and then used for the specified purpose.

3) Data should be adequate, relevant, and not excessive for the specified use.

4) Data must be accurate and, where relevant, kept up to date.

5) Data should not be kept longer than is necessary for the specified purpose.

6) Data processing should meet the legal rights of the data subjects.

7) Data holders should protect the data against loss, theft or corruption.

8) Data should not be transferred abroad, except to certain other European countries.

Q6 a) Software must be installed according to the number and type of licences the individual or user has for the software. Organisations often break the law by installing single-user licensed software on a network or by installing more copies of the software than they are licensed for, (e.g. a company that has 50 licenses for a word processor would break the law if they installed 51 copies of the software).

b) Text and images used on the Internet are subject to copyright, so using them without the permission of the owner or copyright holder is illegal.

c) Copies of computer software can be made as back-ups, in case the original CD is damaged. However if the copy of the software is used to install the software on a machine for which it is not licensed, the person installing the software is breaking the law laid out in the Copyright, Design and Patents Act.

Q7 The three things made illegal by the Computer Misuse Act are:

1) Unauthorised access to a computer system in order to view or copy files.

2) Unauthorised access to a computer system in order to carry out serious crimes like fraud and blackmail (hacking).

3) Unauthorised access to a computer system in order to delete or change files, including planting viruses.

Page 81

Q1 a) iii b) iv c) v d) iv e) ii

Q2

Task	Job Title
Design computer system	Systems analyst
Write computer software	Programmer
Connect computers on a network	Network manager

Q3 In a hot-desking office employees work at any free desk when they come into work.

Q4 Teleworking means the employees can work from home, connecting to the office over the Internet, to upload and download work.

Q5 Advantages:

1) Employers benefit because computers can increase the amount of work done, making businesses more productive.

2) Workers benefit if computers can take over more repetitive tasks.

Disadvantages:

1) It's expensive to invest in computers and it takes time and money to train staff.

2) There may be job losses if computers replace people for some tasks.

Page 82

Q1 a, c

Q2 a) Caused by long-term use of a keyboard or mouse without sufficient rest breaks. Made worse by badly-designed equipment and poor posture.

b) Caused by looking at computer monitors for too long without a break. The glare from monitors and poor quality displays on older monitors can both contribute.

c) Sitting too long on poor quality seating that does not offer sufficient support can lead to back problems, as can a bad posture (slouching in a seat).

Q3 E.g.

1) A proper computer chair, with backrest.

2) An ergonomically-designed keyboard.

3) Good lighting.

4) A screen filter.

Q4 1) Analyse workstations and assess / reduce risks.

2) Ensure workstations meet minimum requirements.

3) Allow employees to plan work so there are breaks or changes of activity.

4) Provide access to free eye tests.

5) Provide health and safety training and information.

Q5 Possible answers:
Poor lighting, bad posture, eyes not level with top of screen.

Page 83

Q1 A social issue is about the effect of something on society / how society is organised. Moral and ethical issues are about whether actions are right or wrong.

Q2 False

Q3 The following types of information are possible answers:
Sexist, racist, ageist, violent, politically extreme, sexually extreme.

Q4 a) It would reduce the amount of offensive / dangerous material on the Internet.

b) Censorship is open to abuse by governments who could prevent access to information they don't want their citizens to have.

Q5 They could be breaking copyright laws, which would be ethically wrong.

Q6 Reducing the number of repetitive jobs could free up people who did those jobs for more interesting work. However there are a limited number of jobs and there is likely to be an overall loss of jobs.

Q7 Advantage:
Some people claim that increased surveillance might help to catch criminals.
Disadvantage:
Many people will object to other people having access to their personal communications and private details — they might see it as an intrusion on their lives.

Page 84

Q1 Computers are expensive and not everyone can afford them. People who have access to computers and the Internet are 'information rich' and people who don't have access are 'information poor'.

Q2 Possible answers:

1) People become less physically fit, because they can communicate with other people (friends, shopkeepers, bankers) without making the effort to go out and see them.

2) People might lose personal skills because they lack practice in dealing with people face to face.

Q3 Some people think that parents who give their children **mobile phones** are making it **harder** for them to become independent and **self-reliant**. There are also worries that increased use of the Internet and **computer games** results in people spending less time **reading**. There is a fear this could lower levels of **literacy**, especially among **young** people.

Q4 Possible answers:

1) Computers make certain jobs easier to do, but as a result workers are expected to get through more work in the same amount of time. Some workers might find this stressful and exhausting. Some might suffer from health problems associated with a lot of computer use.

2) Computer technology is constantly changing and improving. This means workers have to constantly adapt and retrain to use new technology — which is demanding on their time, intelligence and patience.

Q5 a) They reduce the need for workers to travel to work and to conferences. This has the potential to reduce pollution from cars and planes.

b) Viewing information on-screen saves paper, and saves trees.

ISBN 978 1 84762 174 0

9 781847 621740

IHA42